# CHRISTMAS SONGS AND CAROLS FOR GUITAR

Arranged with tablature by
## DAVID NADAL

## DOVER PUBLICATIONS, INC.
Mineola, New York

A graduate of Yale University and the Manhattan School of Music, David Nadal is a frequent performer on both the classical and electric guitar. His recent appearances include the Other Minds Festival in San Francisco, the New York Guitar Festival (with the Sap Dream Electric Guitar Quartet), and a performance with the Glen Branca Ensemble. He has taught at The Juilliard School's Pre-College Division, the Choir Academy of Harlem, and is currently a member of the faculty at LaGuardia Community College and the Amadeus Conservatory in Chappaqua, NY. David is the author of several guitar publications, including his critically acclaimed transcriptions of the complete lute songs of John Dowland (Dover).

*Bibliographical Note*

*Christmas Songs and Carols for Guitar* is a new work, specially compiled and arranged by David Nadal and first published by Dover Publications, Inc., in 2003.

*International Standard Book Number: 0-486-42757-9*

Manufactured in the United States of America
Dover Publications, Inc., 31 East 2nd Street, Mineola, N.Y. 11505

# CONTENTS

Nothing cheers the heart quite like the Christmas carol—familiar, classic, and inextricably intertwined with the joy of the holiday season. Herein lies a collection of twenty-eight new arrangements of old classics for solo guitar. These are arranged in approximate order of difficulty, so the beginner as well as the accomplished guitarist will have no difficulty finding pieces to perform on the concert stage or by the Christmas tree. I hope this collection brings you as much joy as it brought me in preparing it.

David Nadal
*Queens, NY*

# The Gloucestershire Wassail

English traditional carol
arranged by DAVID NADAL

**Merrily and robust**

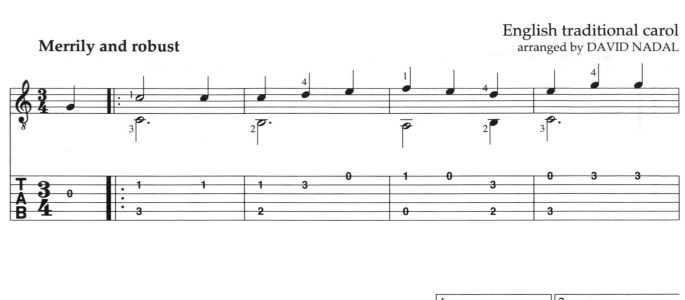

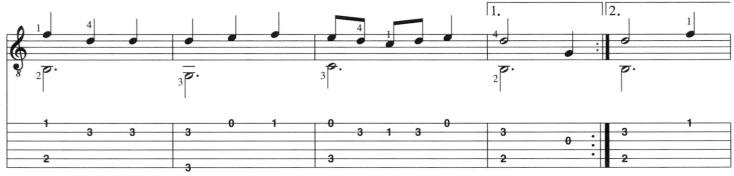

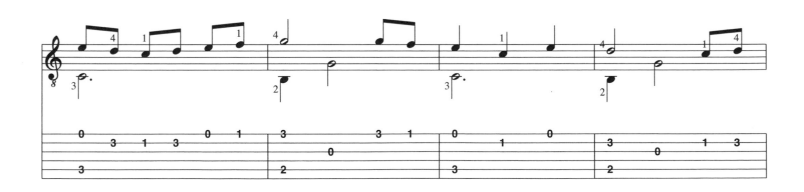

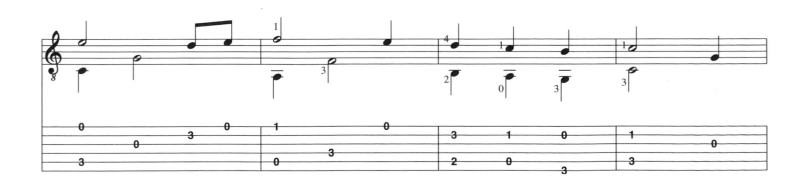

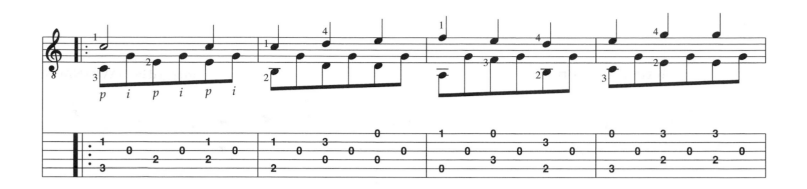

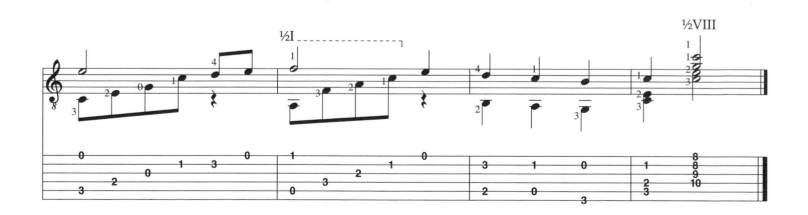

# Jingle Bells

James Pierpont (1857)
arranged by DAVID NADAL

**Bright, quick and energetic**

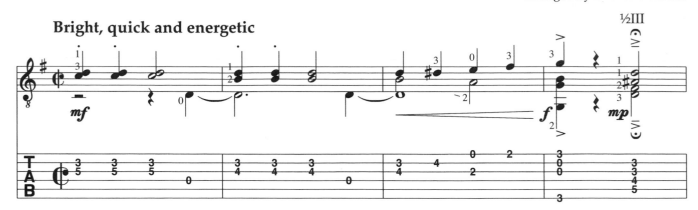

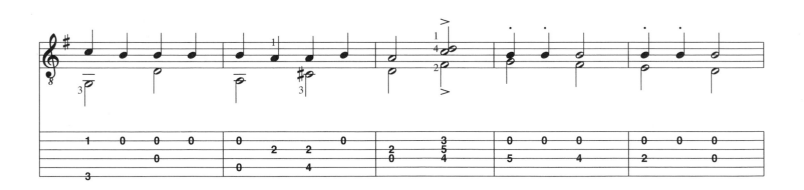

**Fine**

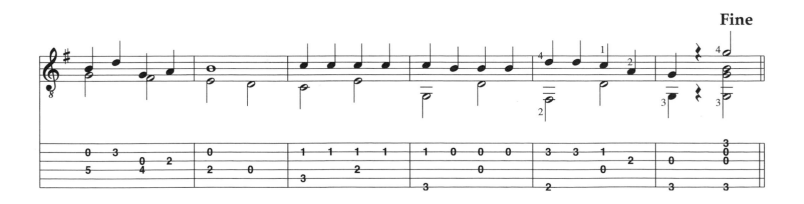

5

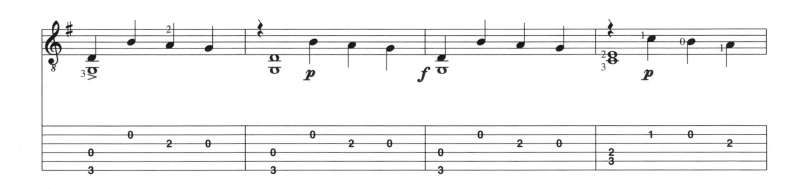

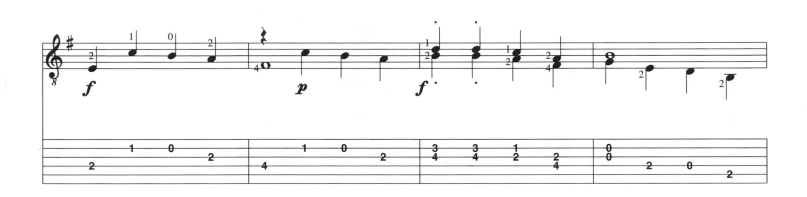

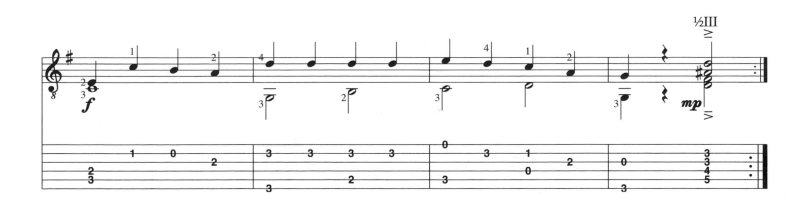

# I Heard the Bells on Christmas Day

Anonymous music set to
words by Longfellow
arranged by DAVID NADAL

**Joyfully, not too fast**

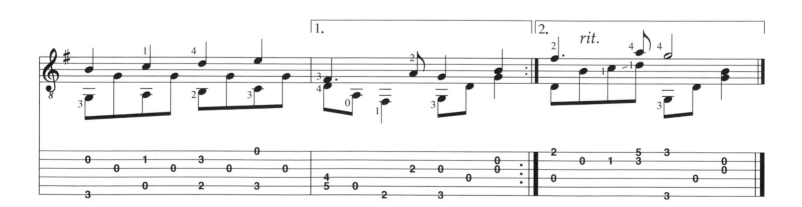

# Once In Royal David's City

Anonymous music set to
words by C.F. Alexander
arranged by DAVID NADAL

**Nostalgically**

# O Little Town of Bethlehem

Lewis H. Redner
arranged by DAVID NADAL

# Deck the Halls

Thomas Oliphant
arranged by DAVID NADAL

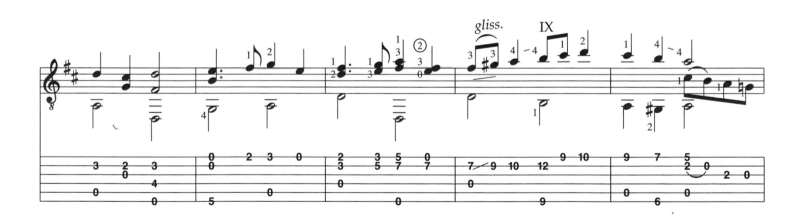

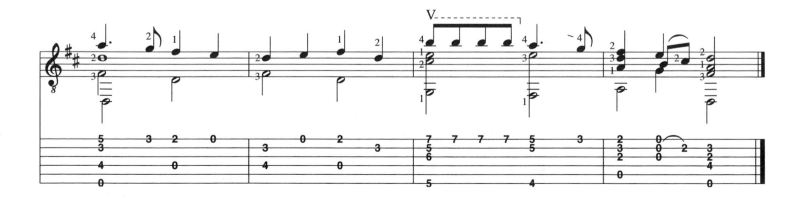

# Here We Come A–Wassailing

English traditional carol
arranged by DAVID NADAL

**With a steady and merry lilt**

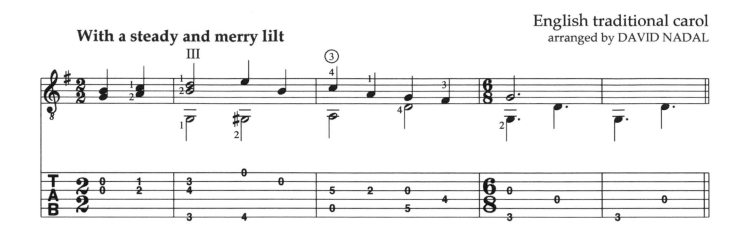

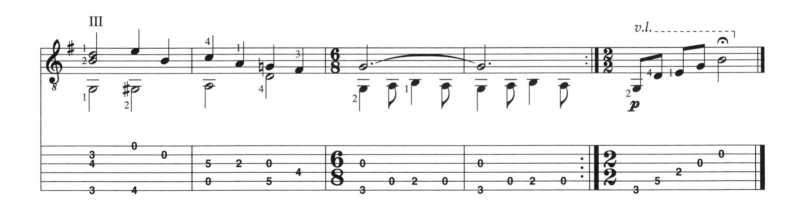

# Angels We Have Heard on High

French traditional carol
arranged by DAVID NADAL

**Joyful and proud**

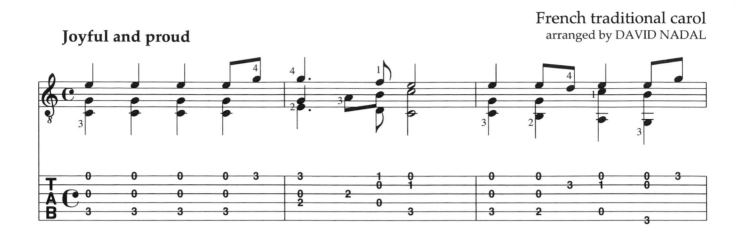

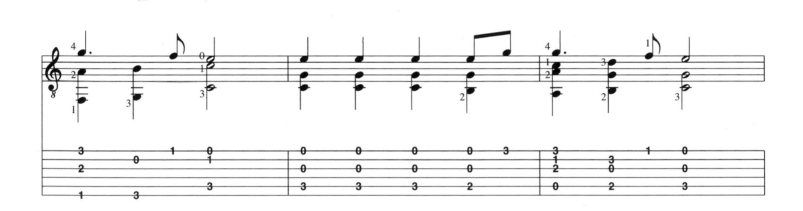

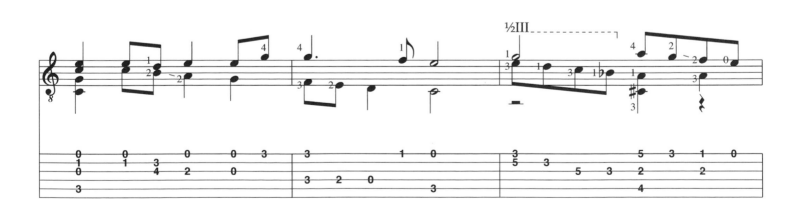

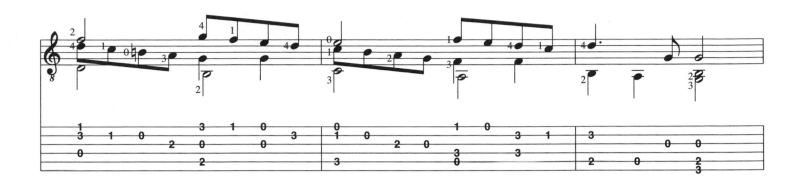

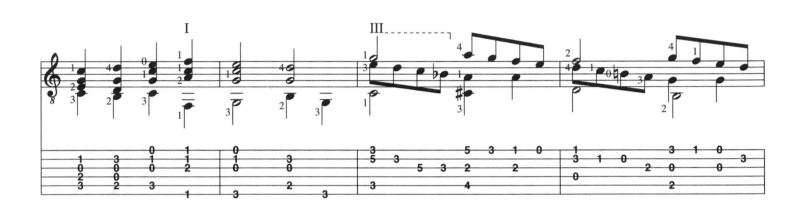

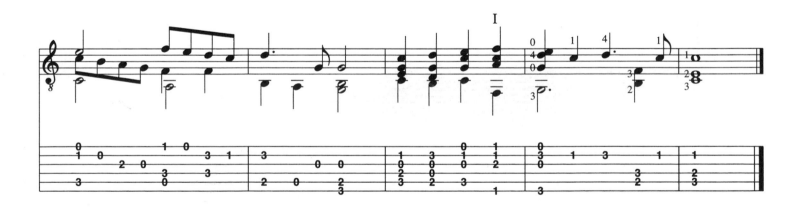

# Good King Wenceslas

Melody from *Piae Cantiones* (1582)
arranged by DAVID NADAL

**Merrily and strong**

# O Christmas Tree

## (O Tannenbaum)

German traditional carol
arranged by DAVID NADAL

**Peacefully**

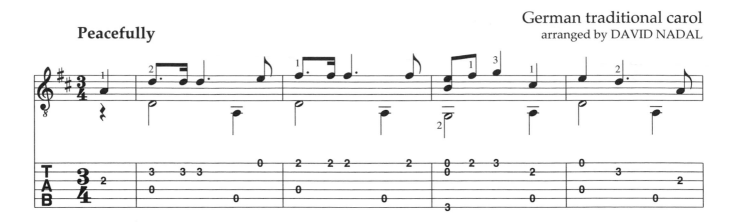

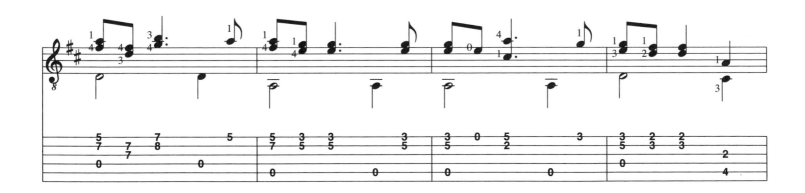

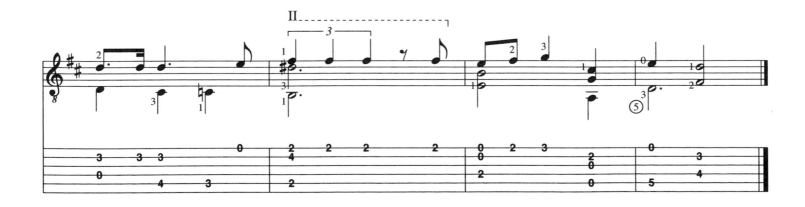

# Hark! The Herald Angels Sing

Felix Mendelssohn
arranged by DAVID NADAL

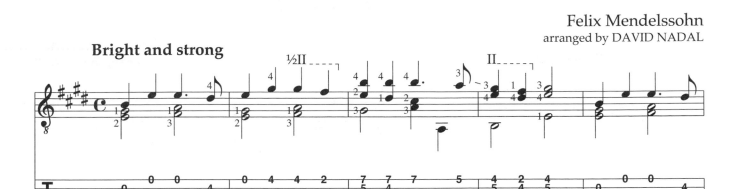

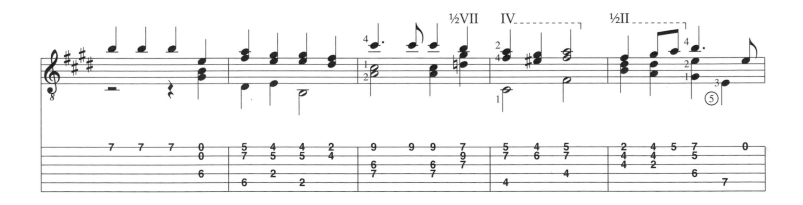

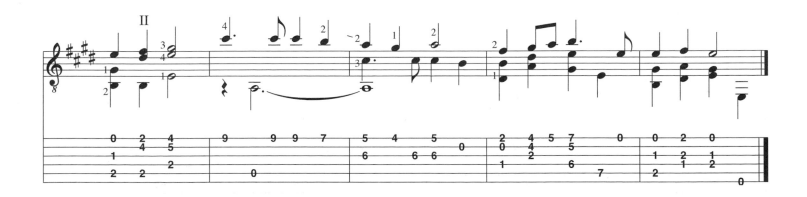

# The Coventry Carol

### (Lully, Lulla)

Anonymous music set to
words by Robert Croo
arranged by DAVID NADAL

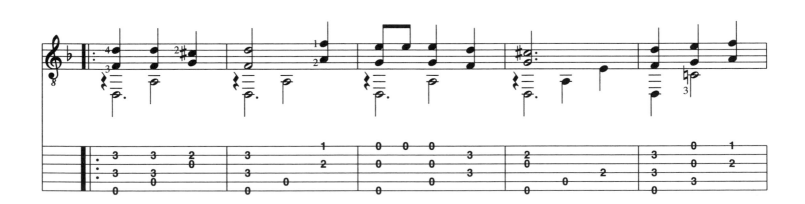

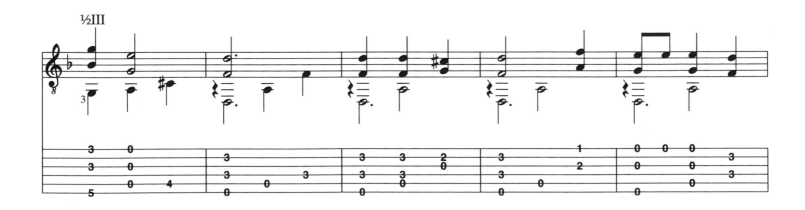

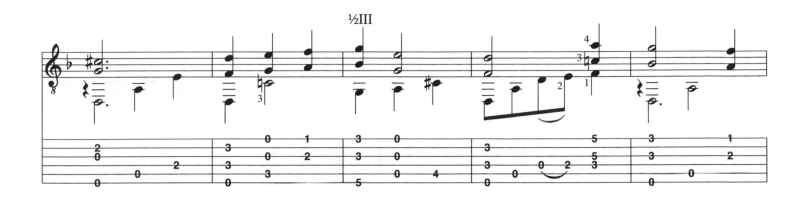

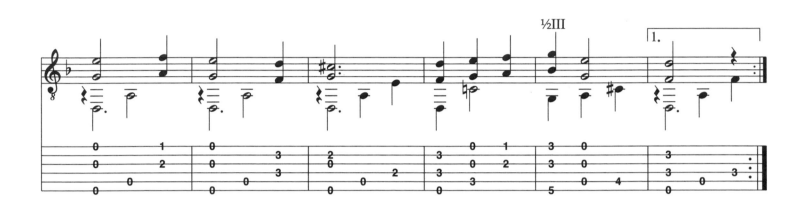

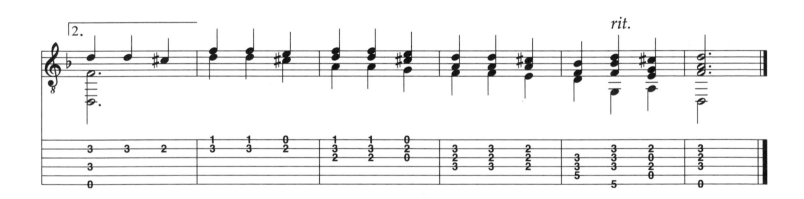

# The Boar's Head Carol

English traditional carol
arranged by DAVID NADAL

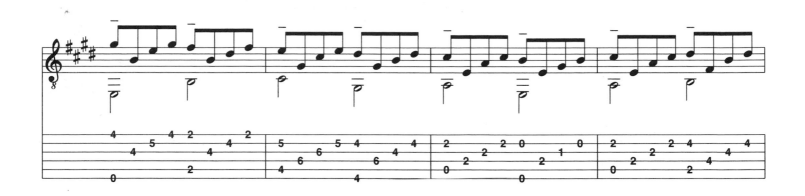

# What Child Is This?

## (Greensleeves)

English traditional carol
arranged by FRANCIS CUTTING
and anonymous others

**With somber simplicity**

**Fine**

# We Wish You a Merry Christmas

English traditional carol
arranged by DAVID NADAL

**Waltz tempo**

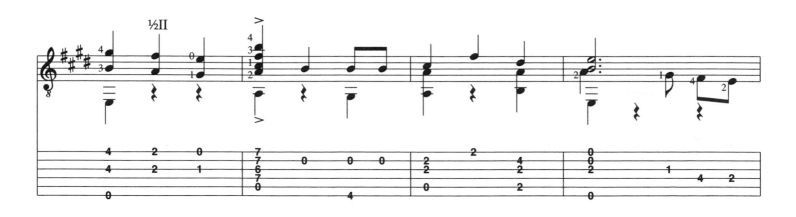

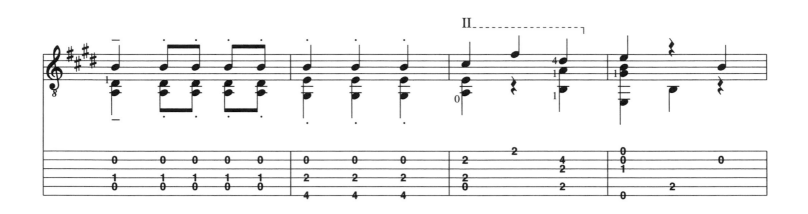

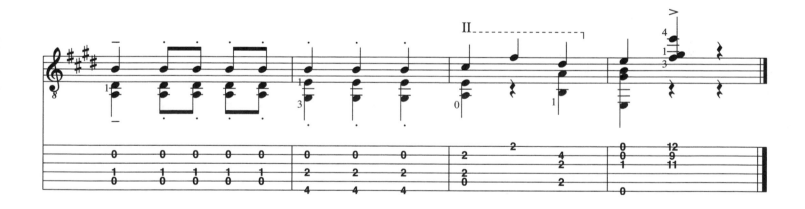

# We Three Kings of Orient Are

John Henry Hopkins, Jr.
arranged by DAVID NADAL

**Graceful and moderately fast**

# Patapan

French traditional carol
arranged by DAVID NADAL

**Quick and rustic**

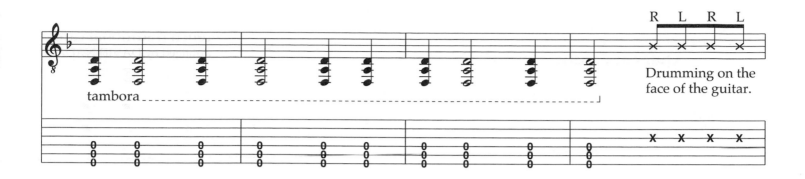

Drumming on the
face of the guitar.

tambora

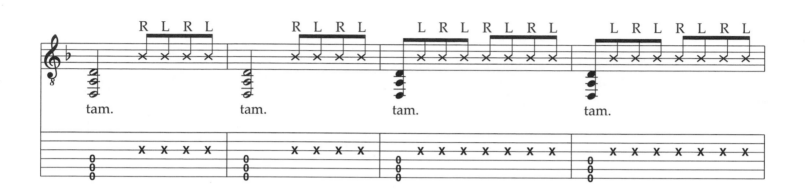

tam.

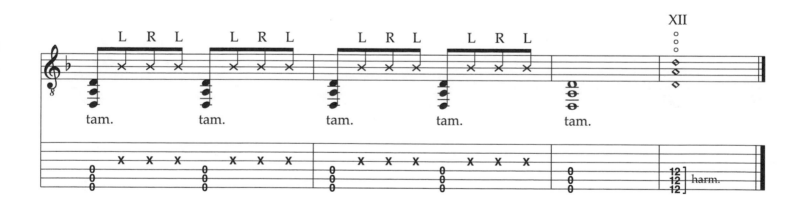

tam.

harm.

# O Holy Night

### (Cantique de Noël)

Adolphe Charles Adam
arranged by DAVID NADAL

**Slowly and majestically**

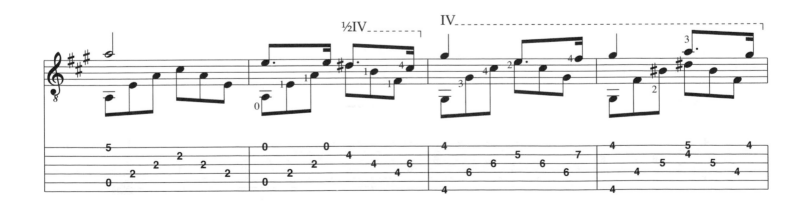

34

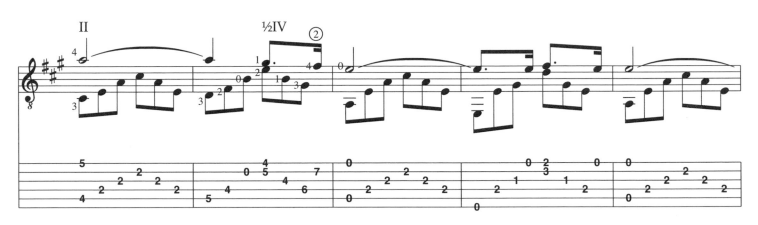

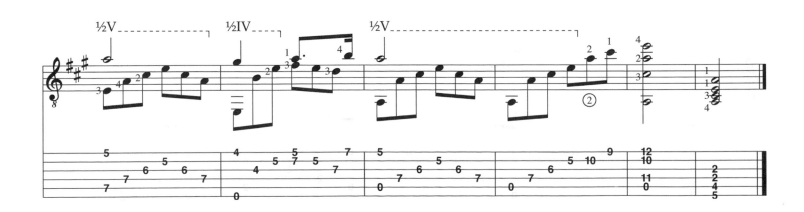

# Away in a Manger

James R. Murray
arranged by DAVID NADAL

**With a tender gracefulness**

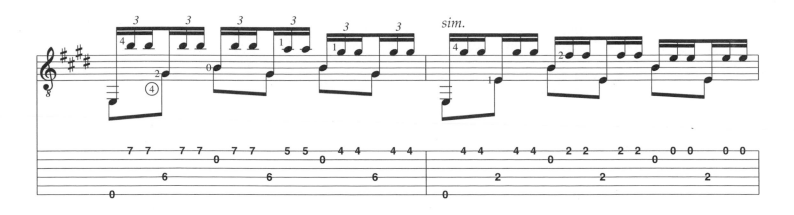

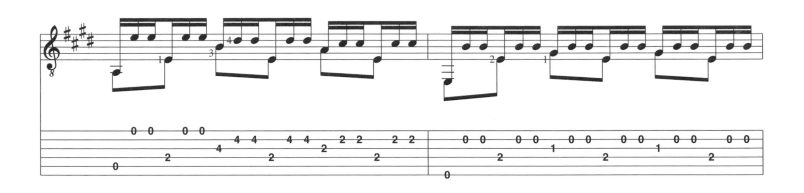

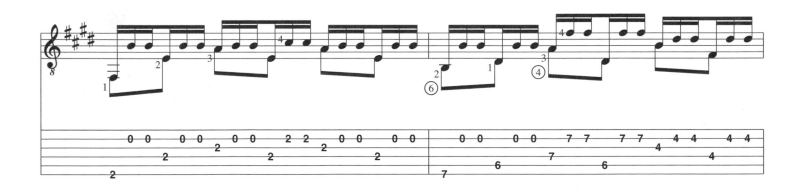

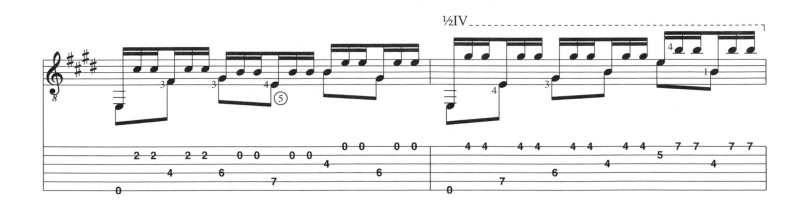

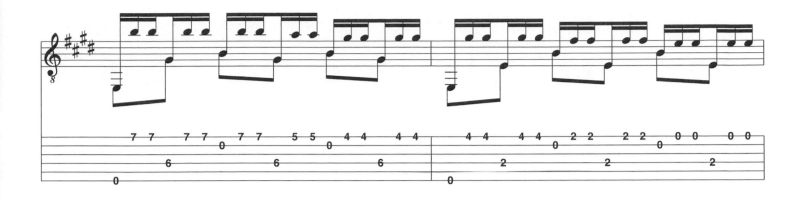

# O Come All Ye Faithful

## (Adeste fideles)

J. Reading
arranged by DAVID NADAL

**Delicately**

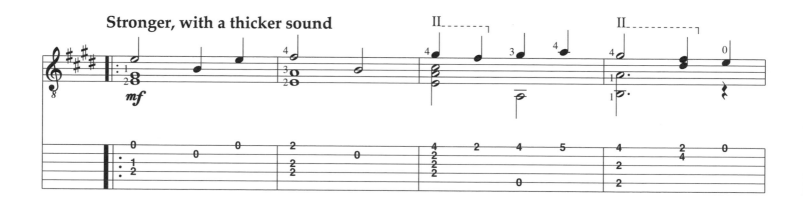

**Stronger, with a thicker sound**

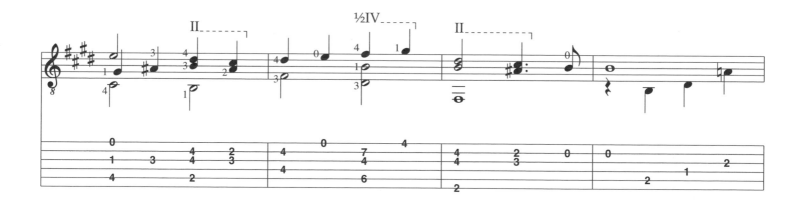

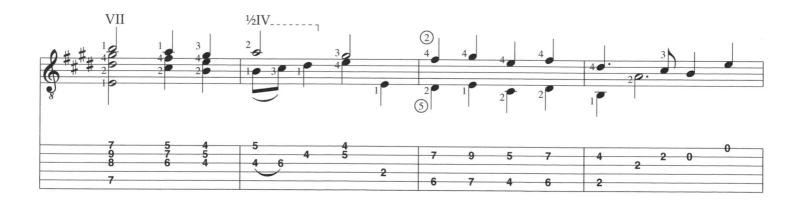

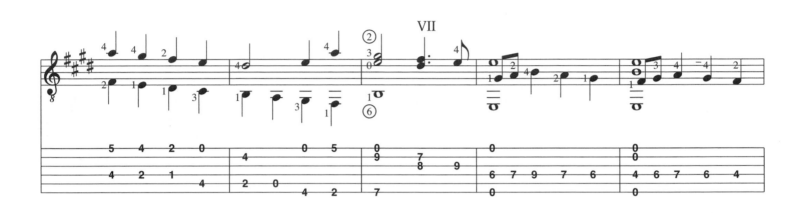

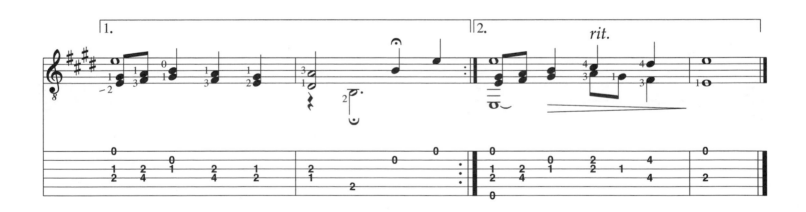

# It Came Upon the Midnight Clear

Richard Storrs Willis
arranged by DAVID NADAL

**Dreamy and nostalgic**

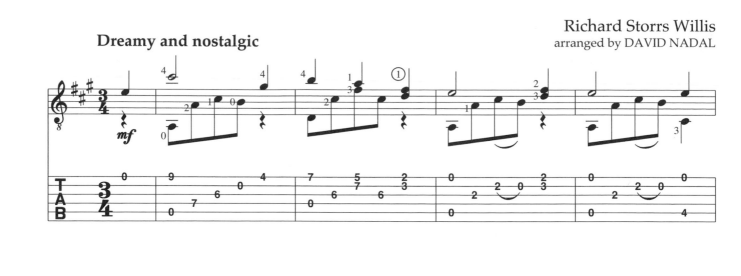

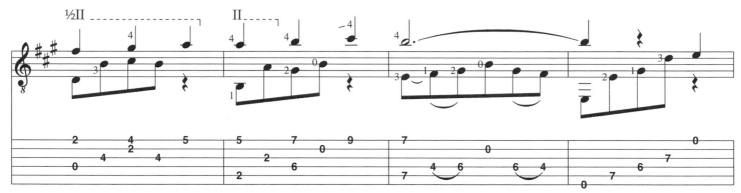

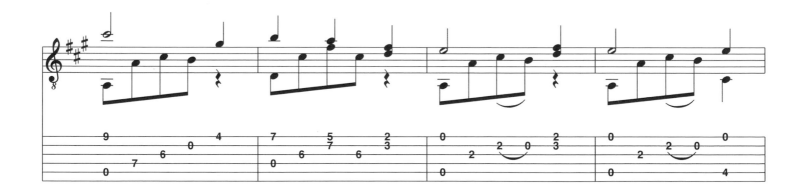

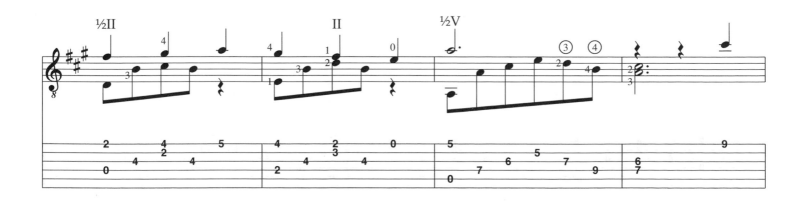

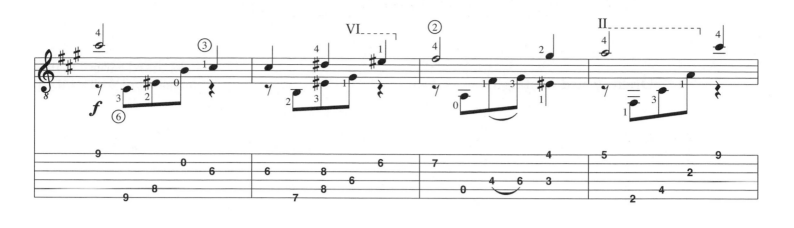

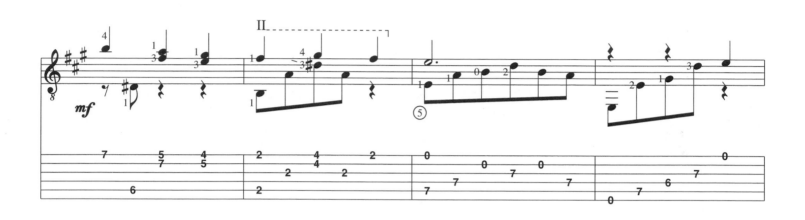

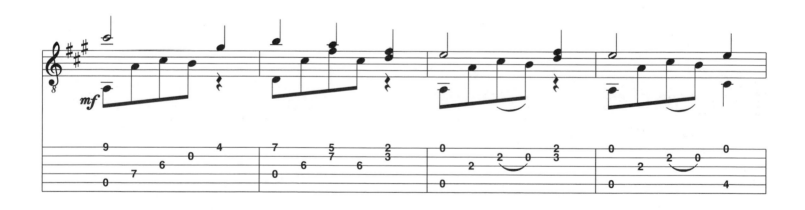

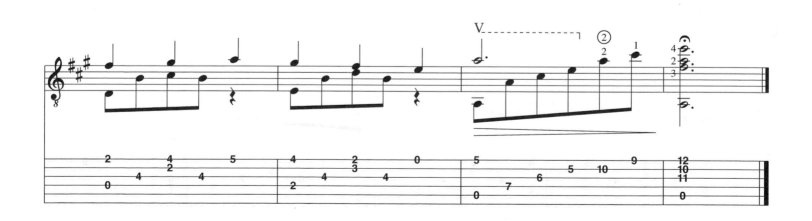

# The Holly and the Ivy

English traditional carol
arranged by DAVID NADAL

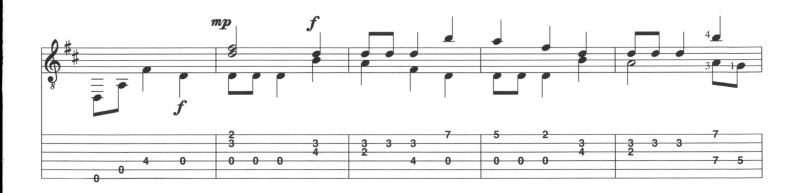

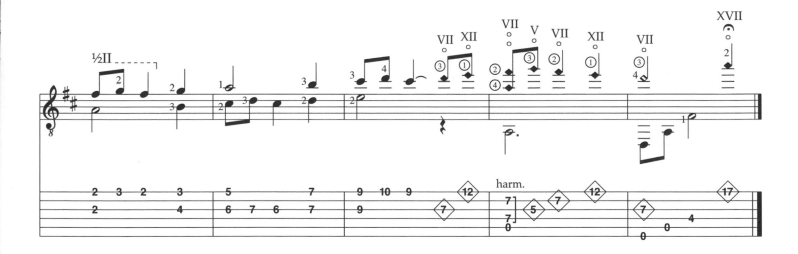

# I Saw Three Ships

English traditional carol
arranged by DAVID NADAL

**Simple and bright**

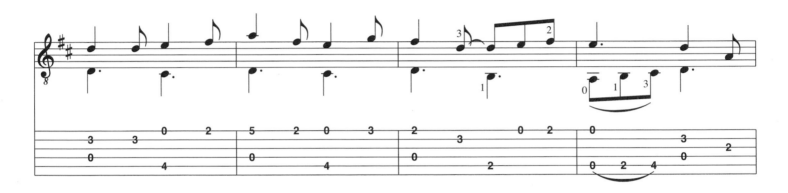

# The First Nowell

English traditional carol
arranged by DAVID NADAL

**Moderately slow, with a strong and sweet sound**

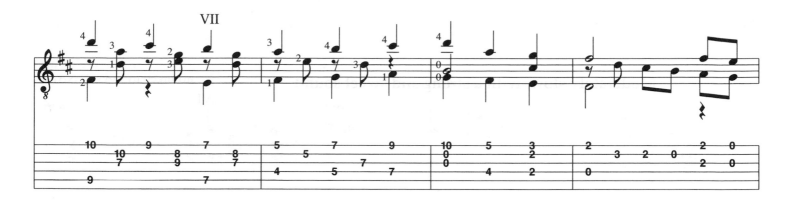

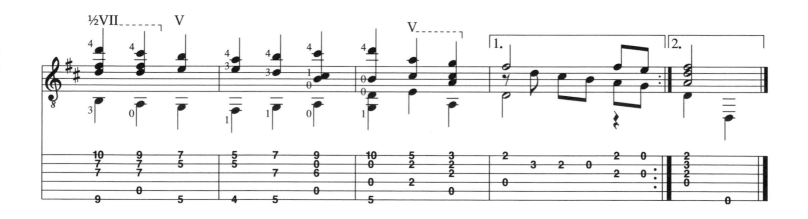

# Silent Night

### (Stille Nacht)

Franz Gruber
arranged by DAVID NADAL

**Quietly lulling**

Play stems up *8va* with artificial harmonics

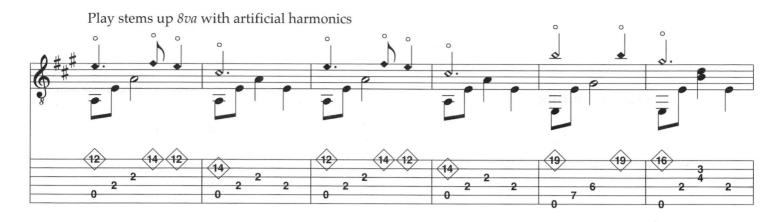

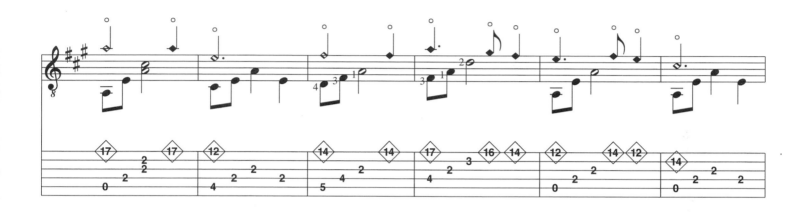

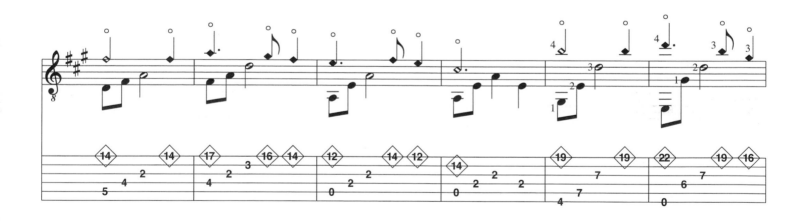

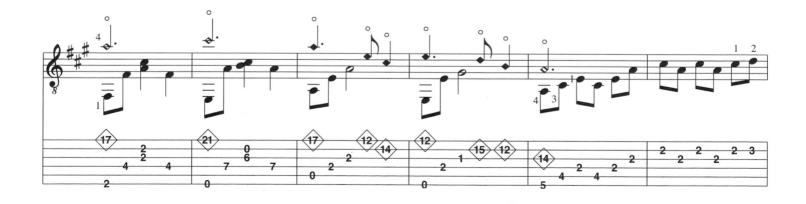

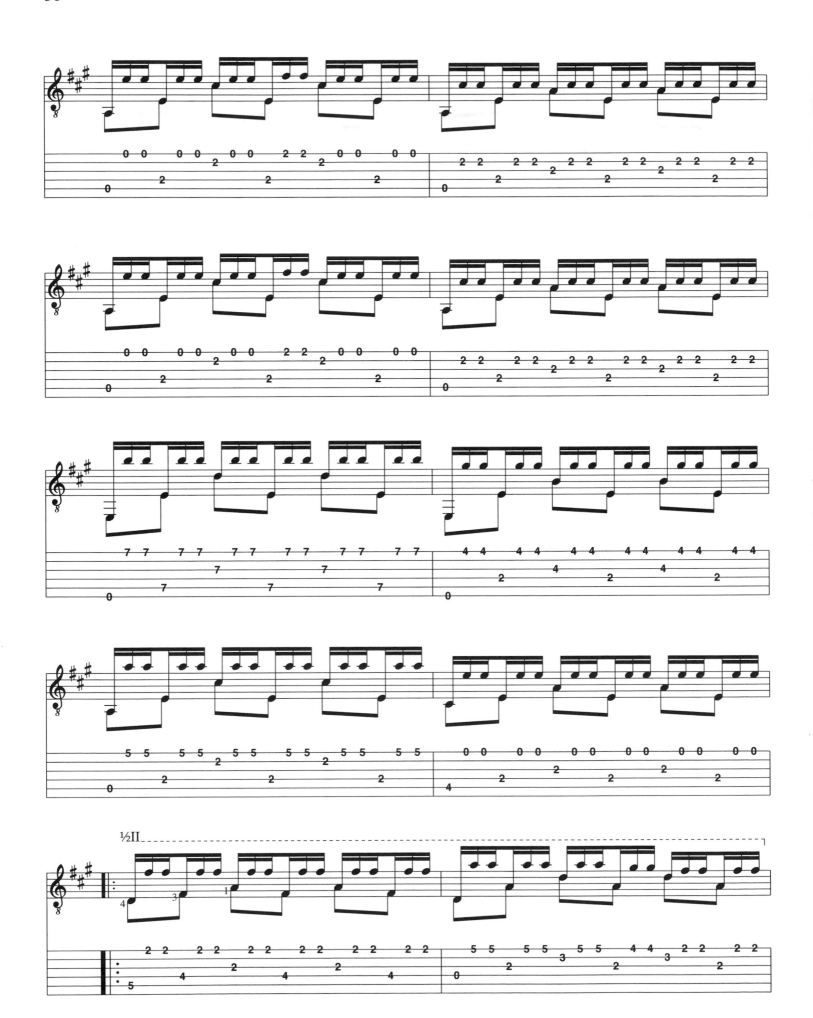

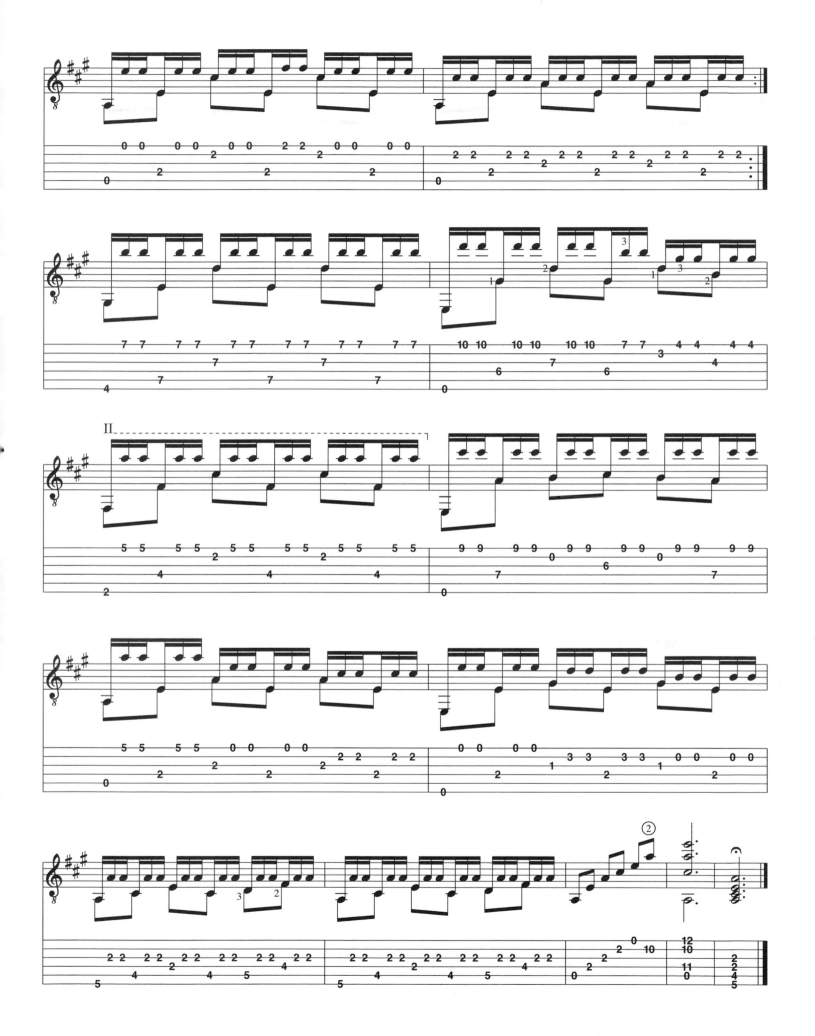

# Masters in This Hall

French traditional carol
arranged by DAVID NADAL

**Somber and at a moderate pace**

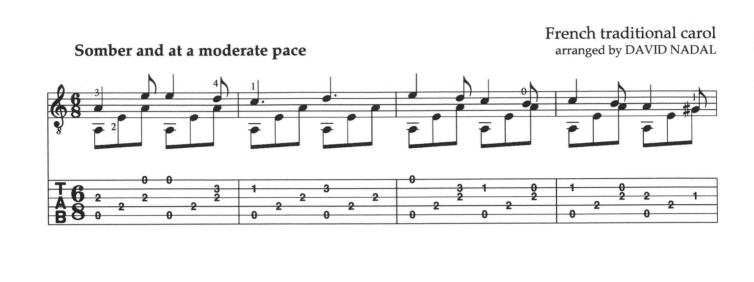

non rit.

Repeat as many times as you wish.

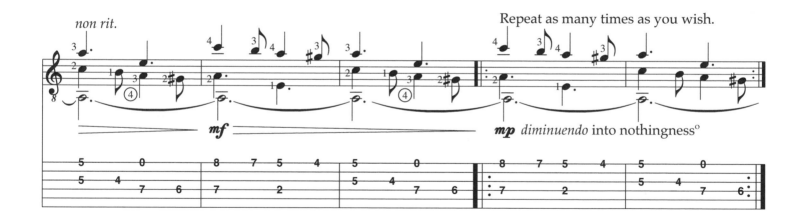

# God Rest Ye Merry, Gentlemen

English traditional carol
arranged by DAVID NADAL

**Somber and steady**

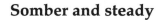

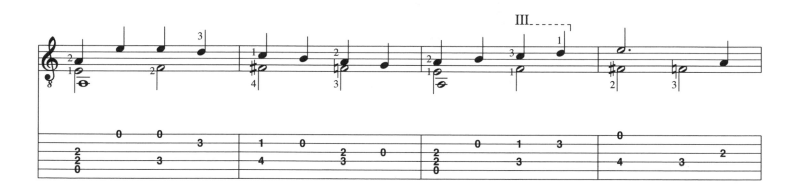

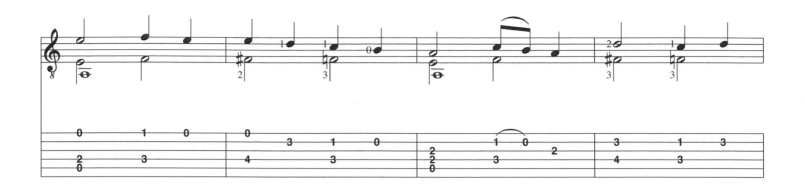

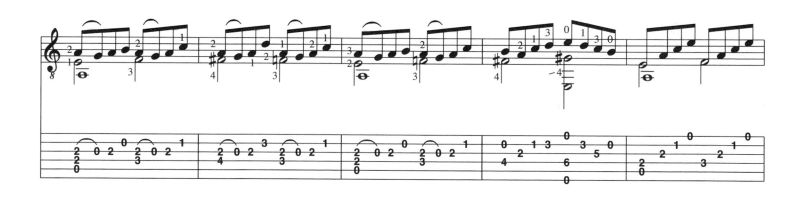

# Joy to the World

Lowell Mason
arranged by DAVID NADAL

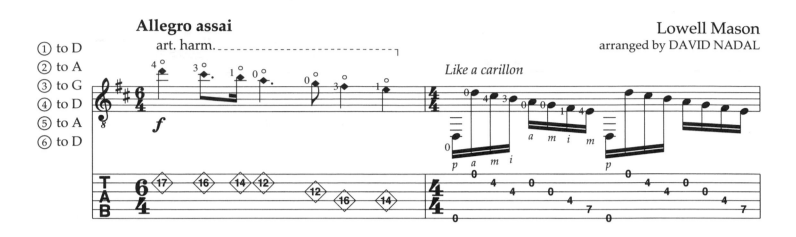

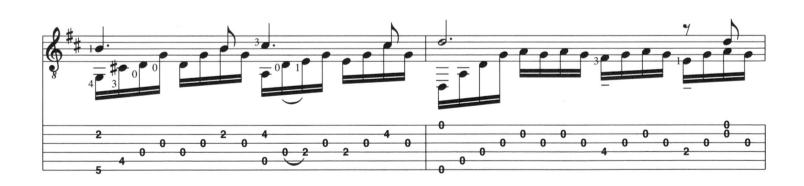

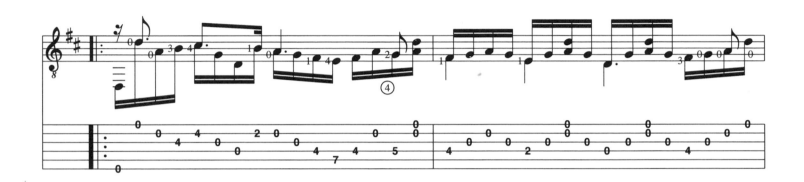

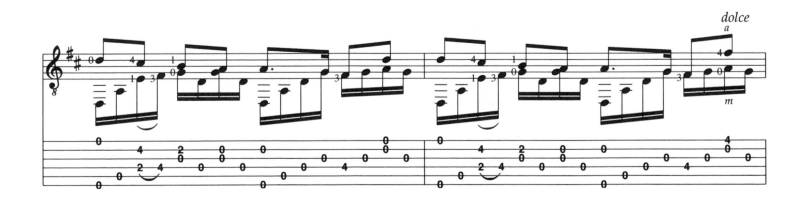

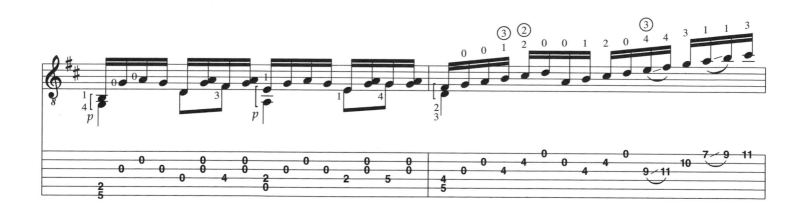

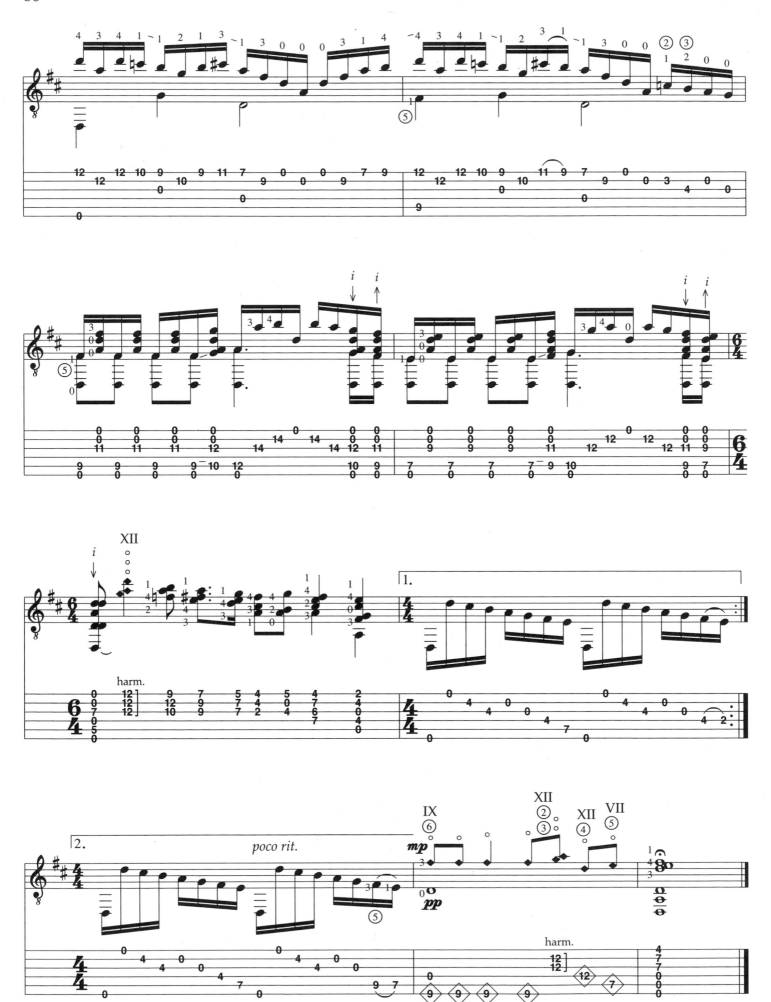